ADWORDS AUTHORITY

ADWORDS AUTHORITY

FINNIAN HAZE

CONTENTS

Introduction	1
1 Setting Up an AdWords Account	5
2 Ad Creation and Optimization	10
3 Targeting and Segmentation	15
4 Monitoring and Analytics	20
5 AdWords Campaign Management	24
6 Advanced Strategies for AdWords Success	29
7 Budget Optimization	34
8 AdWords Policy and Compliance	39
Conclusion	44

Copyright © 2025 by Finnian Haze
All rights reserved. No part of this book may be reproduced in any manner whatsoever without written permission except in the case of brief quotations embodied in critical articles and reviews.
First Printing, 2025

Introduction

In today's digital age, businesses are increasingly engaged in a continuous negotiation to enhance the relevance and visibility of their websites. As the online marketplace grows more competitive, it has become critical for companies to ensure that their websites appear as high as possible on search engine results pages (SERPs) when potential customers search for specific products or services. At present, Google dominates the global search engine market, making it the most influential platform for digital marketing. Securing a top position on Google is arguably the most valuable promotional investment a company can make in this medium.

In 2007, for instance, over 2 million businesses were leveraging Google for marketing purposes. During the same year, internet advertising in the UK surged by 43%, emerging as the most favored advertising medium in an otherwise sluggish market. Remarkably, half of all internet advertising expenditures were allocated to campaigns on Google. This shift underscored the growing importance of performance-driven marketing tools like Google AdWords, which became a cornerstone of the digital advertising landscape. A study by E-consultancy revealed that in 2007 alone, the cost of Google ads increased by 33%. Despite this rise, internet marketing remains a cost-effective medium compared to traditional advertising channels. AdWords, in particular, has been lauded by advertisers as one of the most powerful tools for online marketing. It enables businesses to connect with potential customers through targeted text ads displayed in the top-right corner or above organic search results.

This paper aims to provide actionable guidelines for maximizing the profitability of Google AdWords. It introduces a comprehensive strategy called *AdWords Authority*, which integrates performance goals, keyword selection, system design, campaign initiation, element categorization, and rigorous testing. Developed through extensive personal experience and research, *AdWords Authority* offers a holistic approach to optimizing AdWords campaigns. While adhering to all the guidelines is ideal, businesses are encouraged to implement as many as possible to maximize revenue generation. Ultimately, the effectiveness of these guidelines can only be validated through testing. Readers are advised to test each recommendation within their specific business context to ensure optimal results.

Overview of AdWords

Google AdWords operates much like an auction. Advertisers bid on specific keywords or keyword combinations that trigger the display of their ads. In a traditional auction, the highest bidder wins the item. Similarly, in AdWords, when a user performs a Google search with a keyword phrase that suggests commercial intent, an auction is initiated among advertisers who have bid on that keyword. The participants in this auction are businesses that have paid Google for the opportunity to compete for ad placement.

When using AdWords, advertisers can choose between two primary bidding strategies: broad match and exact match. A *broad match* allows an ad to be displayed for the specified keyword as well as related terms, expanding the potential reach of the campaign. In contrast, an *exact match* ensures that the ad is shown only when the search query precisely matches the chosen keyword, offering greater control over targeting.

Overview of AdWords

AdWords is Google's flagship advertising program, serving as the gateway to placing ads across the Google network. This network includes Google-owned sites like YouTube and Google Maps, as well as partner and affiliated sites. The program supports a wide range of marketing objectives, from building email lists and increasing brand awareness to driving website traffic and facilitating e-commerce transactions.

One of the most compelling features of AdWords is its ability to connect advertisers with users at the exact moment they are actively searching for related products or services. This real-time targeting allows businesses to tap into the searcher's intent, making AdWords a highly effective tool for capturing qualified leads. Compared to organic search engine optimization (SEO), AdWords offers several distinct advantages:

1. **Immediacy of Traffic**: While SEO efforts can take months to yield results, AdWords campaigns can drive traffic to a website almost instantly.
2. **Control Over Positioning**: Advertisers can control where their ads appear on the search results page, ensuring maximum visibility.
3. **Adaptability to Algorithm Changes**: Unlike organic search rankings, which are heavily influenced by Google's ever-changing algorithms, AdWords campaigns are less vulnerable to sudden shifts in search engine policies.

Importance of Google for Businesses

To capitalize on potential and retained sales through their websites, businesses have invested significant resources in attracting highly targeted visitors and optimizing website navigation and functionality. Since a substantial portion of website traffic originates from search engine results pages (SERPs), companies have increasingly focused on improving their visibility and communication on these pages. Enhanced visibility not only drives immediate traffic but also contributes to long-term brand recognition and customer loyalty.

Importance of Google for Businesses

Research on online consumer behavior highlights two key dimensions: informational search and transactional activities. Informational search involves gathering product or service information, while transactional activities result in monetary exchanges. Studies show that search engines, particularly Google, have become indispensable tools for consumers navigating the digital marketplace.

For instance, when consumers trust a specific seller—such as Amazon or eBay—they often use search engines as their primary source of purchase information. Data from generic keyword searches (e.g., "books" or "cell phones") further demonstrates that search engines serve as the starting point for most online shopping journeys. This makes search engines the most frequently visited sites by consumers seeking purchase-related information.

By leveraging Google's advertising tools, businesses can align their marketing efforts with consumer behavior, ensuring that their products and services are visible at critical decision-making moments. This alignment not only drives immediate sales but also fosters long-term customer relationships and brand equity.

CHAPTER 1

Setting Up an AdWords Account

When setting up your Google AdWords account, it's essential to approach it with a clear strategy in mind. Each campaign you create should be tailored to achieve specific goals, whether that's increasing brand awareness, driving sales, or attracting new customers. To maximize the potential of your campaigns, start by identifying your target audience and the outcomes you want to achieve.

For instance, if you're running a local corner store, your primary goal might be to attract new customers who may not yet be aware of your business. Even if your store is well-known in the area, there's always room to grow your customer base. Highlighting promotions and special offers in your ads can be an effective way to draw in new visitors and encourage repeat business. When setting up your AdWords account, be as specific as possible about your objectives. Whether your business is simple or complex, a targeted and specialized approach will yield the best results.

Creating an Account

To begin using Google AdWords, you'll first need to create an account. Start by navigating to the AdWords homepage and clicking on the "Create your first campaign" link, which can be found on the account overview page. Google provides free tutorials and videos through its Learning Center, which can guide you through the setup process. For example, Google uses CarbonFootprint.com as a case study to demonstrate both effective and ineffective AdWords setups.

When creating your account, you'll need to make a few key decisions:

1. **Currency and Time Zone**: Select the currency in which you'll be billed and choose the appropriate time zone for your location. If you manage multiple AdWords accounts, ensure that each one is set to the correct time zone.
2. **Email Address**: Decide which email address you'd like to associate with your AdWords account. Sign in to the Google Account linked to that email address and agree to the terms and conditions to proceed.
3. **Account Management**: If you need to make changes to your AdWords agreement later, you can do so by navigating to the "My Account" page and selecting "AdWords Service."

Once your account is set up, you'll have access to a range of tools and features to help you create and manage your campaigns. If you ever need to create additional accounts, Google allows you to set up up to 15 accounts, including a master/apprentice relationship known as a My Client Center (MCC).

Setting a Budget and Bidding Strategy

One of the most critical steps in setting up your AdWords account is determining your budget and bidding strategy. Your budget will dictate how much you're willing to spend daily on your campaigns, while your bidding strategy will influence how your ads compete in Google's auction system.

1. **Daily Budget**: Start by setting a daily budget that aligns with your financial capabilities. For example, if your daily budget is $10, you might set a maximum-cost-per-click (CPC) bid of $1. This means your budget could be exhausted after 10 clicks, but it also has the potential to generate over 1,000 clicks if your ads perform well.
2. **Bidding Options**: AdWords offers several bidding options, including cost-per-click (CPC), cost-per-thousand-impressions (CPM), and placement targeting. CPC is the most commonly used method, as it allows you to pay only when someone clicks on your ad. This approach is ideal for businesses focused on driving traffic or conversions.
3. **Keyword Bidding**: As you gain more experience with AdWords, you can experiment with different keyword combinations and ad variations to optimize your CPC. For example, you might refine your keywords to include more specific or encouraging phrases that resonate with your target audience. Keep in mind that broad match keywords can expand your reach, but they may also increase your costs if not carefully managed.

Choosing Keywords

The success of your AdWords campaigns hinges on your ability to select the right keywords. Keywords are the foundation of your campaigns, connecting your ads to the search queries of potential customers. A well-chosen keyword strategy can lead to higher sales at a lower cost, while poor keyword selection can waste your budget and yield minimal results.

1. **Relevance and Specificity**: Your keywords should be highly relevant to your products or services and specific enough to attract qualified leads. For example, if you sell handmade leather wallets, using a broad keyword like "accessories" may attract irrelevant traffic. Instead, opt for more specific terms like "handmade leather wallets for men."
2. **Customer Intent**: Think about the intent behind your customers' searches. Are they looking for information, comparing products, or ready to make a purchase? Tailor your keywords to match the stage of the buyer's journey. For instance, someone searching for "best leather wallets" is likely in the research phase, while someone searching for "buy leather wallets online" is closer to making a purchase.
3. **Keyword Match Types**: AdWords offers several keyword match types, including broad match, phrase match, and exact match. Broad match allows your ad to show for related terms, while exact match ensures your ad appears only for the specific keyword you've chosen. Use these options strategically to balance reach and precision.

The Importance of Keyword Selection

Keyword selection is the cornerstone of any successful AdWords campaign. It's the bridge that connects your ads to the needs and queries of your target audience. The better your keywords align with what users are searching for, the more effective your ads will be.

Consider this: users don't have the time or patience to sift through every ad they encounter. If you want to sell a product or service, you need to proactively reach out to potential customers at the exact moment they're searching for what you offer. By mastering keyword selection, you can ensure that your ads are visible to the right people at the right time, ultimately driving more sales and maximizing your return on investment.

CHAPTER 2

Ad Creation and Optimization

Creating and optimizing ads in Google AdWords is both an art and a science. The goal is to craft compelling ads that not only attract clicks but also convert those clicks into meaningful actions, such as purchases or sign-ups. To achieve this, you need to balance creativity with data-driven strategies, ensuring your ads resonate with your target audience while delivering a strong return on investment (ROI).

Calculating ROI and Setting Budgets

Let's start with an example. Suppose you're selling an all-in-one internet marketing tool for $100. If you pay Google $3 per click for your ad, you'd need a 3% conversion rate to break even. While a 33% ROI might seem decent, $3 per click is relatively high. If you're advertising a high-margin product, such as a $600 e-book, the same $3 per click could yield a much higher ROI, especially if your click-through rate (CTR) increases to 3.5%.

However, it's crucial to keep your ad budget in check. A good rule of thumb is to ensure your ad spend doesn't exceed 10% of your expected revenue. For instance, if you expect to sell 10 e-books at 600each,yourtotalrevenuewouldbe600each,yourtotalrevenuewouldbe6,000. Ten percent of that is $600, so your ad budget should ideally stay below this amount. Remember, the ultimate goal isn't just to generate clicks but to drive sales. Even if your CTR is high, a low conversion rate can erode your profitability.

Ad Approval and Launch

Once you've selected your keywords, written your ad copy, and submitted your billing information, your ad will undergo a review process by Google. Typically, ads are approved within a few hours, though it can sometimes take longer. Once your ad is live, focus on monitoring its performance to ensure it delivers a strong ROI. The average ROI for AdWords campaigns is around 50%, but with the right strategies, you can achieve even better results.

Targeting the Right Audience

Creating an ad is only half the battle; the real key to success lies in targeting the right audience. Google AdWords excels in this area, allowing you to reach people who are actively searching for products or services like yours. By leveraging precise targeting strategies, you can ensure your ads are shown to users who are most likely to convert. This not only maximizes your ROI but also minimizes wasted ad spend.

Writing Compelling Ad Copy

Crafting effective ad copy is one of the most critical aspects of AdWords success. With strict character limits, every word must count. Here are some tips for writing ads that convert:

1. **Be Concise and Action-Oriented**: AdWords ads have limited space, so use action-packed language and eliminate unnecessary words. Focus on conveying your message clearly and persuasively.

2. **Highlight Unique Selling Points (USPs)**: Emphasize what sets your product or service apart from the competition. Whether it's a special feature, a limited-time offer, or exceptional customer service, make sure your USPs shine through.
3. **Maintain Integrity**: Avoid overhyped claims or exaggerated promises. Be honest and transparent about what you're offering. Consumers appreciate authenticity, and it builds trust in your brand.
4. **Use Power Words**: Incorporate persuasive language that reassures users they're making the right choice. Words like "exclusive," "limited," and "guaranteed" can create a sense of urgency and exclusivity.

The Nuances of Ad Copy

Small details can make a big difference in ad performance. For example, the placement of an exclamation point, the level of capitalization, or a touch of humility can significantly impact your CTR. Pay attention to these nuances, as they can add up to greater profitability over time.

Ad Extensions

Ad extensions are a powerful tool for enhancing your ads and providing additional information to users. They not only improve the visibility of your ads but also increase the likelihood of clicks. Here are some common types of ad extensions:

1. **Sitelink Extensions**: These allow you to include additional links to specific pages on your website, such as product categories or special offers.
2. **Review Extensions**: Highlight positive reviews or testimonials to build credibility and trust with potential customers.

3. **Call Extensions**: Add a phone number to your ad, making it easy for users to contact you directly.
4. **Location Extensions**: Display your business address, which is particularly useful for local businesses.

By utilizing ad extensions, you can provide more value to users and improve your ad's performance. Google rewards advertisers who offer comprehensive and relevant information, so take advantage of these features to stand out from the competition.

A/B Testing

A/B testing is a proven method for optimizing your ads. By comparing two versions of an ad, you can determine which one performs better and refine your strategy accordingly. Here's how to conduct A/B testing effectively:

1. **Identify a Variable**: Choose one element to test, such as the headline, ad copy, or call-to-action (CTA).
2. **Create Two Ads**: Develop two versions of the ad, changing only the variable you're testing.
3. **Run the Ads**: Let both ads run simultaneously for a minimum of one day (three days is recommended).
4. **Analyze Results**: Compare the CTRs of the two ads. The version with the higher CTR is the winner.

A/B testing allows you to make data-driven decisions and continuously improve your ad performance. Over time, these incremental improvements can lead to significant gains in profitability.

Quality Score

Quality Score is a critical metric in Google AdWords that measures the relevance and quality of your ads, keywords, and landing pages. It directly impacts your ad rank and cost-per-click (CPC). Here's how to improve your Quality Score:

1. **Relevant Keywords**: Ensure your keywords align closely with your ad copy and landing page content.
2. **Compelling Ad Copy**: Write ads that clearly communicate your value proposition and encourage clicks.
3. **Optimized Landing Pages**: Create landing pages that provide a seamless user experience and align with the intent of your ads. Include clear CTAs, relevant content, and easy navigation.
4. **High CTR**: A strong CTR signals to Google that your ad is relevant and valuable to users, which can boost your Quality Score.

By focusing on these factors, you can improve your Quality Score, lower your CPC, and increase your chances of winning ad auctions.

Final Thoughts

Ad creation and optimization are ongoing processes that require attention to detail and a willingness to experiment. By writing compelling ad copy, leveraging ad extensions, conducting A/B tests, and improving your Quality Score, you can maximize the effectiveness of your AdWords campaigns. Remember, the key to success lies in understanding your audience and continuously refining your approach based on data and insights.

CHAPTER 3

Targeting and Segmentation

Targeting and segmentation are foundational elements of any successful Google AdWords campaign. They allow you to focus your efforts on the most relevant audience, ensuring your ads reach the right people at the right time. By understanding and implementing these strategies, you can maximize your return on investment (ROI) and drive meaningful results for your business.

Google's Visibility Segmentation

Until the spring of 2007, businesses and AdWords accounts viewed search results through a framework known as Search Computational Positions (SCPs). These positions represented the average placement of search results, though they didn't account for individual variations within a large dataset. Today, the specifics of SCPs remain confidential to Google, but the concept of visibility segmentation has evolved significantly.

Modern search results are displayed in more than 20 positions, both above the fold (ATF) and below the fold (BTF). In 2004, Google proposed that the 20th position was a sensible BTF position, but this has since been refined based on microeconomic principles. Google now provides frequency distributions that offer deeper insights into how search results are displayed and interacted with. This evolution underscores the importance of understanding visibility segmentation to optimize your ad placements.

Strategic Design: Targeting and Segmentation

The first step in strategic design is defining your target audience and segmenting your market. Targeting involves identifying the key performance indicator (KPI) that measures the business value of a visit. Whether you use G-ROI (Google Return on Investment) or another performance metric, it's essential to track this for every keyword variant. This ensures that you only invest in clicks that generate at least as much profit as they cost.

Segmentation, on the other hand, involves dividing your market into smaller, homogeneous groups. While it's possible to focus on a single segment, most businesses benefit from targeting multiple segments, especially when aiming for growth by tapping into the long tail of search queries.

Geographic Targeting

Geographic targeting allows you to tailor your ads to specific regions, cities, or even neighborhoods. This is particularly useful for businesses with a local or regional focus. Here's how to leverage geographic targeting effectively:

1. **Research Your Audience's Geography**: Use tools like Google News and high-reputation publications to understand where your clients are located. Journalistic niche preparation can provide valuable insights into local trends and preferences.
2. **Analyze Competitive Reports**: Review your AdWords competitive reports and behavior flow data in Google Analytics. Are your searches coming from metropolitan areas? Identify patterns and adjust your targeting accordingly.

3. **Incorporate Geographic Terms**: If your product or service is tied to specific locations, include relevant geographic terms in your keywords. For example, a business offering hiking gear might target keywords like "Rocky Mountain hiking gear" or "Appalachian Trail camping supplies."

Case Study: NatureServe

NatureServe, a non-profit organization, provides taxonomy and data services nationwide. However, their AdWords strategy required a nuanced approach to geographic targeting. By incorporating location-specific keywords and analyzing traffic patterns, they were able to refine their campaigns to better serve their diverse client base. This highlights the importance of tailoring your strategy to your audience's geographic context.

Demographic Targeting

Demographic targeting enables you to reach specific segments of your audience based on factors like age, gender, income level, and interests. This level of precision ensures your ads resonate with the right people, increasing the likelihood of conversions.

1. **Leverage Google's Demographic Tools**: Google provides robust demographic targeting options, allowing you to tailor your ads based on lifestyle and interests. This can significantly reduce click costs and improve ad positioning.
2. **Priority Positioning**: By targeting demographics effectively, you can achieve Priority Positioning, which places your ads in the top few results or on the right-hand side of the page—areas where users are most likely to engage with ads.
3. **Business Intelligence**: Demographic data can also serve as a powerful business intelligence tool. For example, you might discover that most of your online purchases come from a spe-

cific age group or income bracket. This insight can inform broader marketing strategies and product development.

Device Targeting

With the proliferation of mobile devices, device targeting has become an essential component of AdWords campaigns. It allows you to optimize your ads for specific devices, operating systems, and carriers.

1. **Campaign-Level Settings**: AdWords provides campaign-level settings that let you exclude certain carriers or operating systems. This ensures your ads are shown only on devices that align with your target audience's preferences.
2. **Popular Devices List**: Google offers a list of the most popular devices by carrier and operating system. This data can help you refine your targeting and allocate your budget more effectively.
3. **Custom Reports**: Use custom reports to analyze device performance and adjust your targeting accordingly. For example, if you find that users on a specific device model have a higher conversion rate, you can prioritize that device in your campaigns.

Practical Example

Suppose you're running a campaign for a mobile app. By targeting specific devices and operating systems, you can ensure your ads are shown to users who are most likely to download and use your app. This level of precision not only improves your ROI but also enhances the user experience by delivering relevant ads.

Final Thoughts

Targeting and segmentation are critical to the success of your AdWords campaigns. By leveraging geographic, demographic, and device targeting, you can ensure your ads reach the right audience at the right time. These strategies not only improve your ad performance but also provide valuable insights into your market, helping you refine your overall marketing strategy.

CHAPTER 4

Monitoring and Analytics

Effective monitoring and analytics are essential for maximizing the performance of your Google AdWords campaigns. By leveraging tools like Google Analytics and AdWords conversion tracking, you can gain valuable insights into your campaign's effectiveness, optimize your strategies, and ensure a strong return on investment (ROI).

Google Analytics Integration

Google Analytics is a powerful tool that, when integrated with AdWords, provides a comprehensive view of your campaign performance. While AdWords alone can tell you basic metrics like cost, clicks, and click-through rate (CTR), Analytics offers deeper insights into how your campaigns contribute to your website's objectives. Key benefits of integrating Analytics with AdWords include:

1. **ROI Measurement**: Track the ROI of your campaigns by analyzing metrics like conversion rate, value per visit, and e-commerce performance.
2. **Goal Tracking**: Set up goals in Analytics to measure specific actions, such as form submissions, product purchases, or newsletter sign-ups. Mapping these goals to AdWords con-

versions allows you to evaluate the effectiveness of your campaigns.
3. **Behavioral Insights**: Understand how users interact with your website after clicking on your ads. This includes metrics like bounce rate, time on site, and pages per session.
4. **Content Performance**: Identify which pages or sections of your site are driving the most value, enabling you to optimize your content and landing pages.

To make the most of this integration, ensure your Analytics code is properly implemented, avoid dynamic URLs, and maintain high-quality landing pages with metadata and headlines that align with user queries. Avoid unethical practices like using computer-generated traffic or low-quality email campaigns, as these can harm your campaign performance and reputation.

Tracking Conversions

Conversion tracking is the cornerstone of measuring AdWords success. Without it, you're essentially flying blind, unable to determine whether your campaigns are driving meaningful results. Here's how to set up and leverage conversion tracking effectively:

1. **Install Conversion Tracking Code**: Add the AdWords conversion tracking code to your website. This allows you to track specific actions, such as product sales, lead form submissions, or free trial sign-ups.
2. **Define Key Performance Indicators (KPIs)**: Identify the most important metrics for your business, such as sales revenue, lead quality, or customer acquisition cost. Track these KPIs consistently to measure campaign success.
3. **Set Up Sub-Goals**: For international businesses or sites with multiple conversion paths, set up sub-goals to track interme-

diate actions, such as newsletter sign-ups or account creations. These steps build trust and brand awareness, ultimately leading to sales.

The Cost of Not Tracking Conversions

Failing to track conversions is one of the biggest mistakes businesses make with AdWords. Without conversion data, you can't accurately measure ROI or optimize your campaigns. Imagine running an auto repair shop without tracking how many calls result in actual bookings—it's a recipe for financial disaster. The same principle applies to AdWords: if you're not measuring conversions, you're essentially relying on luck rather than strategy.

Performance Metrics

To evaluate and improve your AdWords campaigns, focus on the following key performance metrics:

1. **Conversion Rate**: This is arguably the most important metric. A high conversion rate indicates that your product, pricing, ad copy, and keywords are aligned with user intent. If your conversion rate is low, investigate potential issues like slow website load times or unclear messaging.
2. **Click-Through Rate (CTR)**: CTR measures the ratio of clicks to impressions. A high CTR suggests that your ads are relevant and compelling. It also positively impacts your Quality Score, which can lower your cost-per-click (CPC).
3. **Clicks**: The total number of clicks your ads receive. High click volume indicates strong ad relevance and user interest.
4. **Impressions**: The number of times your ad is displayed. While high impressions can improve brand visibility, it's essential to ensure your ads are shown to the right audience.

5. **Cost**: Keep a close eye on your campaign costs. Low costs relative to revenue indicate a profitable campaign, while high costs may require optimization.

By monitoring these metrics, you can identify areas for improvement and make data-driven decisions to enhance your campaign performance.

Google Analytics Program Participation

For websites generating significant traffic, signing up for Google Analytics is a no-brainer. However, due to the limited number of account invites Google releases, you may need to wait for access. One way to expedite the process is by participating in programs like The Chipmunk Plan + Analytics, where websites share account invites. Participants agree to place Analytics code on their sites, helping each other gain access to the program.

Once you've joined, use Analytics to set goals for every offer or product on your site. Track user behavior throughout their visit and match this data with AdWords performance. For example, by adding URL variables to your AdWords links, you can pass conversion data to Analytics, providing a complete picture of how users interact with your site after clicking on your ads.

Final Thoughts

Monitoring and analytics are critical for the success of your AdWords campaigns. By integrating Google Analytics, tracking conversions, and focusing on key performance metrics, you can gain actionable insights, optimize your strategies, and maximize your ROI. Remember, the goal isn't just to drive clicks—it's to generate meaningful results that contribute to your business's growth.

CHAPTER 5

AdWords Campaign Management

Managing a Google AdWords campaign effectively requires a strategic approach and ongoing attention to detail. By performing key tasks such as monitoring performance, calculating ROI, and optimizing campaign structure, advertisers can maximize the effectiveness of their campaigns and achieve their marketing goals.

Key Tasks for Campaign Management

1. **Monitoring and Adjusting**:
   Once your AdWords campaign is live, continuous monitoring is essential. Advertisers must track performance metrics such as click-through rate (CTR), conversion rate, and cost-per-click (CPC). Based on these insights, adjustments can be made to improve results. For example, you might tweak keyword bids, refine ad copy, or test different landing pages. Hiring a professional team to manage your campaign can be a worthwhile investment, especially for complex or high-budget campaigns.

2. **Calculating Return on Investment (ROI):**
   ROI is a critical metric for evaluating the success of your AdWords campaigns. It measures the profitability of your advertising spend by comparing the revenue generated to the cost of the campaign. The formula for ROI is:

$$ROI = \frac{(Revenue - Ad\ Spend)}{Ad\ Spend} \times 100$$

For instance, if you spend $1,000 on a campaign and generate $2,000 in revenue, your ROI is 100%. This means you've doubled your investment. Regularly calculating ROI helps you determine whether your campaigns are delivering value and where adjustments are needed.

1. **Designing and Implementing Ads:**
   Well-crafted ads can attract visitors to your site automatically, making your business visible to your target audience. AdWords allows companies to display ads when users search for relevant products or services, even if the business doesn't have its own website. Google's solutions providers can create a simple site and ad at a low cost, making it accessible for small businesses to compete effectively.
2. **Cost Management:**
   One of the advantages of AdWords is the ability to monitor and control advertising costs in real time. Advertisers can set daily budgets, adjust bids, and pause underperforming campaigns to ensure they stay within budget while maximizing results.

Campaign Structure

A well-structured campaign is the foundation of AdWords success. Here's how to organize your campaigns for optimal performance:

1. **Ad Groups**:
   Create at least six ad groups per campaign, each targeting a specific set of keywords. This allows you to test different ad variations and identify the best-performing combinations. Google's algorithms will automatically optimize for the highest-performing ads.
2. **Match Types**:
   Separate broad match, phrase match, and exact match keywords into different ad groups. This makes it easier to analyze performance data and optimize your campaigns effectively. A randomized structure with mixed match types can obscure insights and hinder optimization.
3. **Compact and Targeted Ad Sets**:
   Keep your ad sets focused and specific. By concentrating on tightly defined audiences, you can manage your campaigns more efficiently and achieve better results. Avoid the temptation to combine multiple ad sets within a single campaign; instead, run one ad set per campaign to simplify optimization.

Ad Scheduling

Ad scheduling allows you to control when your ads are shown, ensuring they are visible to your target audience at the most effective times. Here's how to implement ad scheduling effectively:

1. **Understand Customer Habits**:
   Analyze your audience's behavior to determine the best times to run your ads. For example, if your customers are most ac-

tive during weekday evenings, schedule your ads to run during those hours.

2. **Test and Optimize**:
Start with an aggressive schedule, running ads throughout the day, and then refine based on performance data. Use the "pod schedule" method to test different times and identify the most profitable periods.

3. **On-Peak Scheduling**:
Focus your ad activity during peak times when customers are most likely to convert. This approach maximizes ROI by concentrating your budget on high-performing periods.

4. **Turn Off Ads on Less Profitable Days**:
If certain days consistently underperform, consider pausing your ads during those times to save costs and reallocate your budget to more profitable periods.

Ad Placement

Ad placement is a critical factor in the success of your AdWords campaigns. By leveraging Google's Display Network, you can customize where and how your ads are shown to potential customers. Here's how to optimize ad placement:

1. **Targeting Options**:
Use keywords, specific site URLs, topics, demographics, and interests to target your ads effectively. This ensures your ads are shown to the most relevant audience, increasing the likelihood of engagement and conversions.

2. **Contextual Matching**:
Google's algorithms evaluate the content, images, URLs, and structure of publisher sites to determine the best placements

for your ads. By aligning your ads with relevant content, you can improve their performance and relevance.
3. **Engage Customers at Every Stage**:
Use the Display Network to reach customers at different stages of the buying process, from awareness to consideration and purchase. This approach helps build brand loyalty and encourages repeat business.
4. **Travel Network**:
If your business operates in the travel industry, participating in Google's travel network can enhance your visibility. This network provides opportunities to showcase your ads alongside relevant travel content, increasing your reach and impact.

Final Thoughts

Effective AdWords campaign management requires a combination of strategic planning, continuous monitoring, and data-driven optimization. By focusing on key tasks like ROI calculation, ad scheduling, and ad placement, you can maximize the performance of your campaigns and achieve your marketing objectives. Remember, the goal is not just to drive traffic but to generate meaningful results that contribute to your business's growth.

CHAPTER 6

Advanced Strategies for AdWords Success

To truly excel with Google AdWords, you need to go beyond the basics and implement advanced strategies. These techniques can help you optimize your campaigns, improve ROI, and stay ahead of the competition. From conversion tracking and bid management to remarketing and dynamic search ads, these strategies are essential for maximizing the potential of your AdWords campaigns.

Conversion Tracking: Identifying Valuable Keywords

One of the most critical aspects of AdWords management is determining which keywords are driving conversions and which are simply draining your budget. Conversion tracking allows you to measure the effectiveness of your keywords by tracking specific actions, such as purchases, newsletter sign-ups, or form submissions. Here's how to use conversion tracking effectively:

1. **Set Up Conversion Tracking**: Install the AdWords conversion tracking code on your website to monitor user actions. This data will help you identify which keywords are driving valuable traffic.

2. **Analyze User Behavior**: Look beyond conversions to understand how users interact with your site. Metrics like pages per session and time on site can provide additional insights into keyword performance.
3. **Weed Out Underperformers**: Keywords that don't convert or engage users should be paused or adjusted. Focus your budget on high-performing keywords that deliver measurable results.

Why Some Clicks Don't Convert

Even if your ads receive frequent clicks, they may not always lead to sales. This could be due to factors like irrelevant ad copy, poor landing page experience, or mismatched user intent. Regularly reviewing and optimizing your campaigns can help address these issues.

PPC Bid Management: Staying Agile

Pay-per-click (PPC) bid management is not a one-time task—it requires ongoing attention and adjustment. Consumer behavior and market conditions can change rapidly, impacting the performance of your keywords. Here's how to stay agile with bid management:

1. **Monitor Keyword Performance**: Track the performance of your keywords daily or weekly. Identify trends and adjust your bids accordingly.
2. **Adjust for Market Changes**: As new products or campaigns launch, consumer interest may shift. Be prepared to update your keyword portfolio to reflect these changes.
3. **Leverage Automation**: For campaigns with hundreds or thousands of keywords, consider using third-party AdWords

tools. These platforms can automate bid adjustments, saving you time and improving efficiency.

Remarketing: Re-Engaging Lost Visitors

Remarketing is a powerful strategy that allows you to re-engage users who have previously interacted with your website. By targeting these users with tailored ads, you can increase conversions and maximize ROI. Here's why remarketing works:

1. **Higher ROI**: Remarketing campaigns often deliver a 7x return on ad spend (ROAS) by targeting users who are already familiar with your brand.
2. **Dynamic Remarketing**: This advanced form of remarketing displays ads featuring the exact products or services a user viewed on your site. By showing personalized ads, you can significantly increase conversion rates.
3. **Audience Segmentation**: Remarketing allows you to segment your audience based on their behavior, such as cart abandoners or frequent visitors. Tailor your ads to each segment for maximum impact.

Privacy Considerations

While remarketing is highly effective, it's important to balance personalization with privacy. Ensure your campaigns comply with data protection regulations and respect user preferences.

Dynamic Search Ads: Automating Ad Creation

Dynamic Search Ads (DSAs) are a unique feature of AdWords that automatically generate ads based on the content of your website. This approach is particularly useful for businesses with frequently changing inventory or large product catalogs. Here's how DSAs work:

1. **Automated Keyword Selection**: Instead of manually selecting keywords, DSAs scan your website and use its content to determine relevant search terms.
2. **Relevant Ad Copy**: Google generates ad headlines and descriptions based on the most relevant content from your site, ensuring your ads align with user queries.
3. **Flexibility and Control**: While DSAs automate much of the process, you can still set parameters to control which pages are included and how ads are displayed.

When to Use DSAs

DSAs are ideal for businesses with dynamic content, such as e-commerce sites or news platforms. However, they may not be suitable for campaigns requiring strict control over ad messaging.

Display Network Advertising: Expanding Your Reach

Google's Display Network allows you to showcase your ads on millions of websites, apps, and videos across the internet. This expansive reach makes it an excellent platform for building brand awareness and driving conversions. Here's how to make the most of Display Network Advertising:

1. **Dynamic Remarketing**: Use dynamic remarketing to display personalized ads featuring products users previously viewed on your site. This approach can significantly boost click-through rates (CTR) and conversions.
2. **Targeting Options**: Leverage advanced targeting options, such as demographics, interests, and topics, to ensure your ads reach the right audience.
3. **Visual Appeal**: Display ads are highly visual, so invest in high-quality images and designs to capture user attention.

Benefits of Display Network Advertising

- **Lower Costs**: Display ads often have a lower cost-per-click (CPC) compared to search ads.
- **Higher Engagement**: Visual ads can be more engaging than text-based ads, making them ideal for brand-building campaigns.
- **Retargeting Opportunities**: The Display Network is a powerful platform for remarketing, allowing you to re-engage users who have already interacted with your brand.

Final Thoughts

Advanced AdWords strategies like conversion tracking, bid management, remarketing, dynamic search ads, and Display Network advertising can take your campaigns to the next level. By leveraging these techniques, you can optimize your ad spend, improve ROI, and stay competitive in the ever-evolving digital landscape. Remember, the key to success lies in continuous testing, analysis, and adaptation.

CHAPTER 7

Budget Optimization

Effective budget management is the backbone of any successful Google AdWords campaign. Without proper optimization, you risk overspending on underperforming keywords or missing out on opportunities to scale high-performing ones. Here's a structured approach to budget optimization that ensures your campaigns deliver maximum ROI.

The Budget Optimization Cycle

1. **Set a Consistent Budget Release Schedule**:
   Allocate a fixed amount of your budget weekly or monthly, depending on your campaign goals and cash flow. Over time, you'll identify the optimal frequency for releasing funds based on performance data.
2. **Monitor Keyword Performance**:
   Regularly review how your keywords are performing. Some keywords may drain your budget without delivering results, while others may be nearing their spending limits. Pause or adjust underperforming keywords to reallocate funds to more profitable ones.
3. **Avoid Budget Blowouts:**
   One of the biggest pitfalls in AdWords is overspending early

in the day, leaving no budget for potential high-converting clicks later. Use daily budget caps and automated rules to prevent this issue.
4. **Analyze Campaign Results**:
Before allocating your budget, analyze the performance of previous campaigns. Identify trends, such as which keywords drive the most conversions or which ad groups have the highest ROI. Use this data to inform your budget allocation decisions.

Cost-Per-Click (CPC) Optimization

CPC optimization is a critical component of AdWords management. By focusing on the right keywords and bid strategies, you can reduce costs while maximizing conversions.

1. **Build Tight Keyword Groupings**:
Group keywords into tightly themed ad groups to ensure relevance and improve Quality Scores. For example, if you sell hiking gear, create separate ad groups for "hiking boots," "backpacks," and "camping tents."
2. **Focus on Relevance**:
Ensure your ads are directly relevant to the keywords they target. Irrelevant ads lead to wasted clicks and higher costs. Use dynamic keyword insertion (DKI) to tailor ad copy to user searches.
3. **Bid Strategically**:
While a higher bid can improve ad position, it doesn't always guarantee better results. Focus on keywords with a proven track record of conversions and adjust bids based on performance data.

4. **Leverage Automated Bidding**:
   Use Google's automated bidding strategies, such as Target CPA (Cost-Per-Acquisition) or Enhanced CPC, to optimize bids in real time. These tools use machine learning to adjust bids based on historical performance and conversion data.

Ad Rank Improvement

Ad Rank determines where your ad appears on the search results page. It's calculated based on your bid, Quality Score, and expected impact of ad extensions. Here's how to improve your Ad Rank and achieve better ad positions:

1. **Use Automated Bidding Tools**:
   Automated bidding tools like Target CPA and Target ROAS (Return on Ad Spend) can help you achieve your acquisition goals while maintaining a competitive ad position. These tools require at least 30 conversions in the past 30 days to function effectively.
2. **Track Performance with Analytics**:
   Use Google Analytics to monitor which keywords and ad groups are driving sales, leads, or other conversions. Tools like dynamic value insertion can provide insights into the revenue generated by specific keywords, helping you refine your bidding strategy.
3. **Improve Relevance and Authority**:
   Relevance is determined by how well your ad and landing page align with the user's search intent. To improve relevance:
   - Include the keyword phrase in your ad headline and description.
   - Ensure your landing page is fast-loading, descriptive, and easy to navigate.

◦ Avoid intrusive pop-ups or irrelevant content.
4. **Enhance Landing Page Experience**:
   A high-quality landing page not only improves Ad Rank but also boosts conversions. Focus on creating engaging, original, and user-friendly landing pages that align with your ad messaging.
5. **Leverage Ad Extensions**:
   Ad extensions, such as sitelinks, callouts, and structured snippets, can improve your Ad Rank by increasing ad relevance and click-through rates. Use extensions to provide additional information and encourage users to take action.

Advanced Strategies for Ad Rank Improvement

1. **Linked In-Market and Affinity Audiences**:
   Use in-market and affinity audiences to target users who are actively researching or have shown interest in products or services similar to yours. This cross-channel attribution strategy can improve ad relevance and drive higher-quality traffic.
2. **Smart Display and Gmail Campaigns**:
   Leverage Google's Smart Display campaigns and Gmail ads to reach users across multiple touchpoints. These campaigns use machine learning to optimize ad placements and bidding strategies, ensuring maximum ROI.
3. **Data-Driven Attribution**:
   Implement data-driven attribution models to understand the customer journey and allocate credit to the most impactful touchpoints. This approach helps you optimize bids based on actual conversion paths rather than last-click attribution.
4. **Maintain a Higher Ad Position**:
   A higher ad position typically results in a higher click-through

rate and better conversions. Achieve this by combining competitive bids with high-quality ads and landing pages. Continuously optimize your campaigns to maintain or improve your Ad Rank.

Final Thoughts

Budget optimization, CPC management, and Ad Rank improvement are interconnected strategies that form the foundation of a successful AdWords campaign. By monitoring performance, leveraging automation, and focusing on relevance, you can maximize your ROI and achieve your marketing goals. Remember, AdWords is not a "set it and forget it" platform—continuous testing, analysis, and adaptation are key to long-term success.

CHAPTER 8

AdWords Policy and Compliance

Adhering to Google AdWords policies is not just a formality—it's a critical aspect of running successful campaigns. Violating these policies can lead to disapproved ads, suspended accounts, and even permanent bans. To avoid these pitfalls, it's essential to understand and comply with Google's guidelines. This section outlines key policies, common violations, and best practices to ensure your campaigns remain compliant.

Key AdWords Policies

Google's AdWords policies are designed to maintain a safe, trustworthy, and positive experience for users. Here are some of the most important policies to keep in mind:

1. **Prohibited Content**:
    - **Weapons and Ammunition**: Ads promoting the sale of weapons, ammunition, knives, or related accessories are strictly prohibited.
    - **Illegal Substances**: Ads for illegal drugs, prescription drugs without a prescription, or content related to drug use are not allowed.

- **Adult Content**: Ads containing adult or explicit material, including pornography, are banned. This applies to both ad text and landing pages.
- **Explosives and Pyrotechnics**: Ads promoting fireworks, explosives, or similar products are not permitted.
- **Misleading Claims**: Ads must not contain false or exaggerated claims about products or services.

2. **Restricted Content**:
   - **Alcohol**: Ads for alcohol must comply with local laws and target appropriate audiences.
   - **Gambling**: Gambling-related ads are allowed only in certain regions and must adhere to specific guidelines.
   - **Healthcare and Medicines**: Ads for healthcare products or services must comply with local regulations and Google's policies.

3. **Editorial and Technical Requirements**:
   - **Ad Format**: Ensure your ads use correct grammar, spelling, and punctuation. Avoid excessive capitalization, symbols, or exclamation points.
   - **Landing Pages**: Landing pages must be functional, relevant, and provide a positive user experience. Avoid under-construction pages or misleading redirects.
   - **URLs**: Use properly formatted URLs that accurately reflect the destination page.

4. **Respect for User Experience**:
   - **Offensive Content**: Ads must not contain content that is likely to offend users, including hate speech, violence, or discriminatory material.

- **Spiritual and Religious Content**: Ads referencing spiritual or religious themes must be relevant to the product or service being promoted.

Common Compliance Mistakes

Even experienced advertisers can inadvertently violate AdWords policies. Here are some common mistakes to avoid:

1. **Keyword Stuffing**: Overloading your ad text with keywords can lead to disapproval. Focus on creating clear, concise, and relevant ads.
2. **Misleading Offers**: Ads must accurately represent the product or service being promoted. Avoid exaggerated claims or false promises.
3. **Poor Landing Page Quality**: Landing pages must be functional, fast-loading, and aligned with the ad's messaging. Avoid pop-ups or intrusive elements that disrupt the user experience.
4. **Adult Keywords**: Even if your ad doesn't contain explicit content, using adult-related keywords can lead to disapproval.

Consequences of Non-Compliance

Failing to comply with AdWords policies can have serious consequences, including:

1. **Ad Disapproval**: Google may disapprove ads that violate its policies, preventing them from running until the issues are resolved.
2. **Account Suspension**: Repeated violations can lead to account suspension, halting all campaigns and forfeiting any unused budget.

3. **Permanent Ban**: In severe cases, Google may permanently ban an account, prohibiting the advertiser from using AdWords in the future.

Proactive Compliance Tips

- **Stay Updated**: Google's policies evolve regularly. Stay informed by visiting the AdWords Policy Center and AdWords Support Center.
- **Test Before Launching**: Use the AdWords Policy Manager to check your ads for compliance before launching them.
- **Monitor Performance**: Regularly review your campaigns for potential policy violations, such as high click-through rates (CTR) on disapproved ads.

Ad Content Guidelines

Creating high-quality, compliant ad content is essential for campaign success. Here's how to ensure your ads meet Google's standards:

1. **Accurate Information**:
    - Ensure the age rating, product details, and pricing in your ads are accurate.
    - Landing pages must match the ad's content and provide a seamless user experience.
2. **Professional Quality**:
    - Use high-quality images, videos, and text that reflect your brand's professionalism.
    - Avoid low-resolution or poorly designed creatives.
3. **Language and Tone**:

- Use clear, respectful, and appropriate language in your ads.
- Avoid offensive or inflammatory content.
4. **Creative Value**:
    - Focus on creating ads that provide value to users, such as informative content or compelling offers.
    - Avoid generic or repetitive messaging.

Final Thoughts

Compliance with Google AdWords policies is not just about avoiding penalties—it's about building trust with your audience and creating a positive advertising ecosystem. By following these guidelines, you can ensure your campaigns are effective, ethical, and aligned with Google's standards. Remember, staying compliant is an ongoing process that requires vigilance, adaptability, and a commitment to quality.

Conclusion

As we reach the end of this exploration into the intricacies of Google AdWords and advanced digital marketing strategies, it's clear that success in this dynamic field requires a blend of creativity, precision, and adaptability. The journey through campaign management, budget optimization, compliance, and advanced strategies has illuminated the importance of aligning your efforts with both technical best practices and the ever-evolving expectations of your audience.

The Power of Strategic Alignment

The true value of your AdWords campaigns lies not just in their ability to generate clicks or conversions, but in their capacity to create meaningful connections with your audience. Like the "energetic power" described in the metaphorical "spiritual Cities," your campaigns can achieve a synergistic flow when all elements—keywords, ad copy, landing pages, and targeting—work in harmony. This alignment transforms individual efforts into a cohesive force, driving measurable results and long-term growth.

Embracing Anti-Entropic Principles

In the context of digital marketing, the concept of "anti-entropy" can be seen as the continuous effort to bring order, efficiency, and purpose to your campaigns. By applying the strategies and insights shared in this guide, you can counteract the natural tendency toward chaos and inefficiency, ensuring your campaigns remain focused, effective, and impactful. This anti-entropic approach not only enhances performance but also fosters a culture of collaboration and innovation within your team.

The Role of Free Will and Initiative

Just as the "Inexorable" force described in the text serves as a catalyst for individual initiative and collective progress, your commitment to mastering AdWords empowers you to take control of your marketing destiny. By leveraging the tools and techniques at your disposal, you can navigate the complexities of digital advertising with confidence and creativity. This sense of agency is what transforms challenges into opportunities and drives sustained success.

A Call to Action

As you move forward, remember that the journey of optimization is never truly complete. The digital landscape is constantly evolving, and so too must your strategies. Stay curious, stay adaptable, and continue to refine your approach based on data, feedback, and emerging trends. Whether you're a seasoned marketer or just beginning your AdWords journey, the principles outlined in this guide will serve as a foundation for growth and innovation.

Final Thoughts

In the end, the true measure of your success lies not in the metrics alone, but in the impact you create—for your business, your audience, and your team. By embracing the lessons of this guide and applying them with intention and integrity, you can unlock the full potential of Google AdWords and achieve results that are both transformative and enduring.

www.ingramcontent.com/pod-product-compliance
Lightning Source LLC
LaVergne TN
LVHW041640070526
838199LV00052B/3466